The "Walking Stick" Method of Self-Defence

The "Walking Stick" Method of Self-Defence

"an officer of the Indian Police"

Paladin Press • Boulder, Colorado

The "Walking Stick" Method of Self-Defence
by "an officer of the Indian Police"

Copyright © 2004 by Paladin Press

ISBN 13: 978-1-58160-438-2
Printed in the United States of America

Published by Paladin Press, a division of
Paladin Enterprises, Inc.,
P.O. Box 1307
Boulder, Colorado 80306 USA
+1.303.443.7250

Direct inquiries and/or orders to the above address.

PALADIN, PALADIN PRESS, and the "horse head" design are
trademarks belonging to Paladin Enterprises and registered in United
States Patent and Trademark Office.

Visit our website at www.paladin-press.com.

CONTENTS

PUBLISHER'S NOTE

The following reprint is a faithful representation of the book *The "Walking Stick" Method of Self-Defence*, published c. 1923. In order to preserve the work in its original form, all figure references appear exactly as they did in the original text. Figure placement is, at times, unconventional when compared to modern martial arts books, so careful study of the text and figures is required if this reprint is to be used for training purposes.

PREFACE

There is nothing like novelty. The jaded appetite can be whetted anew by a new dish; the jaded mind by a new occupation.

Public opinion has nowadays been glutted to satiety with literature on all manners of self-defence; and these have been, and are being, dished up again and again, with here a touch of change and there a spice of variety.

In this little book there is offered a complete change of diet.

To acquire proficiency in Boxing, Wrestling, and Ju-Jitsu, demands a certain expenditure of strenuous effort and money; more than the average man is prepared to concede.

The Walking Stick method of self-defence demands none.

The only appliance necessary is that possessed by nearly all; no special clothing or equipment is wanted; no, or little training. It can be learnt in quite a short time without strenuous exercise. *It can be acquired by men, women and children indiscriminately.* Yet it is essentially scientific. And this, combined with its simplicity, should suit exactly the average present-day man.

A walking stick is probably the only weapon the ordinary person is likely to have in his possession when attacked. How many know how to use it to its best advantage? How many even know that a method exists whereby a harmless and cherished ornament can become a sure and powerful stand-by in time of stress and peril?

So far as is known, there is yet no other publication on the subject running on standardised lines. The System has been carefully built up after several years' thought and demonstration, and combines a method devised by a Frenchman, Vigui, of which little is now heard, together with the stick play of tribes of negroes on certain of the West India Islands, called "Bois." Additions and ameliorations have been made as the result of experience and close practise under varying circumstances. The favourable reception of the method by police officials and others in the Bombay Presidency and elsewhere (copy of letters and reports appear further on) as well as the keenness displayed by a certain Boy Scout Troop in India, first gave rise to the idea of general publication; and it is confidently hoped that novelty, utility, and facility will form a combination which will not fail to attract public attention.

The idea is novel; even the illustrations are novel, and show, better than words, how the method is being received in India.

As far as Boy Scouts, and other kindred organisations are concerned, the exercises will speak for themselves and show how eminently suitable they are from both a hygienic and practical point of view. In fact, the rising generation, ever on the lookout for the new and the useful, can confidently be expected to take up the method with whole-hearted vigour.

Some Reports and Expressions of Opinion

(Copy of para. 46 of the Annual Report of the Administration of the Bombay Presidency Police, 1921).

DRILL.—In spite of vacancies and the heavy demands made on the force at different times, the drill of the force of the Presidency Proper and Sind continues to be satisfactory.

Special attention has been paid to training the men in the use of the "heavy cudgel." It is probable, however, that the "heavy cudgel" will in the course of time be supplanted by a light ash plant. A Frenchman who had incurred the enmity of the Apaches in Paris extricated himself on several occasions from a dangerous situation by vigorously attacking his assailants *with his umbrella*; seeing the possibilities of a short and comparatively light weapon in the hands of a man skilled in its use, he perfected a system of "stick-defence." Mr. Lang, Superintendent of Agency Police, Kathiawar, studied this system while on leave, and has trained a number of policemen in Kathiawar since his return. The men seem to take naturally to the art and have proved themselves to be apt pupils. Selected men from other districts are being sent to Kathiawar for training, and in the course of time the new method of defence will be taught in each district. The principle underlying the system of stick defence is that man is a comparatively easily vulnerable animal and that a heavy bludgeon is not needed to incapacitate him; a light and handy weapon, therefore, in the hands of a trained man gives him the advantage of speed over the untrained man armed with the heavy bludgeon such as is usually affected by the rioter.

(Copy of letter No. 480/G. 41-17, dated 19/20-1-1923, from the Commissioner of Police, Calcutta).

In connection with paragraph 46 of the Annual Police Report of the Bombay Presidency for 1921, I would be grateful if you would obtain for me details of the system of training policemen in the use of "lathis"⋆ mentioned as having been introduced by Mr. Lang, Superintendent of Police, Kathiawar. Such training would be very valuable to our men here.

(No. 11771 of 1923. Police Department, Office of the D.I.G. of Police, Karachi, dated the 1st December, 1923).

Memorandum.

LATHI PRACTISE.—With reference to his No. 3976,

⋆ General term for stick.

dated the 11th October, 1922, the District Superintendent of Police, Kathiawar, is requested to let the undersigned know if he can undertake the training of two men from Sind in Lathi★ Practise. The date on which the men should arrive at Rajkot and the officer to whom they should report may please be intimated.

Sd./D. G. OMMANNEY,
Deputy Inspector-General of
Police for Sind, Karachi.

To the District Supdt. of Police,
Kathiawar, Rajkot.

(Below U.O.R. No. 4853, dated 1st May, 1923, From the Inspector-General of Police, Bombay Presidency, Poona).

Returned with compliments.

2.—The only experience in this city is that of the Lathi★. It has served its purpose, but the constabulary make a very crude use of it, and no Lathi Drill is taught.

3.—Mr. Lang's practical illustrations of the efficiency of the stick as a means of attack have persuaded us *that it is a more convenient weapon and one that is far more formidable in the hands* of a man trained to its use.

Sd./F. E. SHARPE,
For Commissioner of
Police, Bombay.

(Copy of No. SAP. 1/3/22/17, dated the 24th April, 1923, from the Commissioner of Police, Kantoor Van de Kommissaris, Pretoria, to the Inspector-General of Police, Bombay Presidency, Poona).

★ Stick.
★ Here means cudgel.

I have the honour to inform you that I have perused with much interest the information given under the heading "Drill," wherein the use of light sticks as weapons of defence and offence for police purposes is mentioned, contained in paragraph 46, page 34, of your Police Report for 1921.

I will be much obliged to receive full particulars of the stick in use, i.e., length, thickness and weight, etc, and also the detail and other useful information appertaining to the drill or system adopted.

(Copy of letter from the Private Secretary to His Excellency Sir George Ambrose Lloyd, G.C.I.E., D.S.O., Governor of Bombay).

Office of the Private Secretary
to the Governor of Bombay,
Government House,
Ganeshkhind, Poona.
23rd July, 1923.

His Excellency wishes me to write and compliment you on the demonstration which you gave of the methods you had devised for the employment of a walking stick as a weapon of offence and defence.

His Excellency was much impressed with what he saw, and considers that you will be doing most valuable service by perfecting and completing the system you have evolved.

(Copy of letter dated 13th July, 1923, from His Highness Maharaja Sir Ghanshyamsinhji, Raj Saheb of Dhrangadhra, G.C.I.E., K.C.S.I.)

I had occasion to witness a demonstration of a new art introduced by Mr. H. G. Lang in the Agency Police of the use of the Walking Stick for purposes of self-defence and was vastly impressed by the performance. *It is really amazing how an ordinary walking stick can be made to serve as a very effective weapon of offence and defence.* I consider it an undoubtedly useful art which it would be worth while for *every man to learn.* As the organiser of the first Boy Scouts in Kathiawar, I was at once struck with the possibility of introducing it into the training of the Scouts with advantage, and to that end have specially deputed my Director of Scouts to acquire a thorough and practical knowledge of the system.

(Copy of letter dated 4th July, 1923, from Lieut.-Colonel W. M. P. Wood, C.I.E.).

I am glad to hear that you are publishing a book on the use of a walking stick for the purposes of self defence.

The little I saw in one day's exhibition of stick play impressed me immensely. *It showed one clearly what a good defensive and offensive weapon a walking stick could be.* My impression was that any man in a crowd armed with nothing else than a walking stick could not only give a very good account of himself but could also keep a considerable number of men at bay for some time and also considerably damage them. The combined play, too, was most effective.

I wish you all success. If I can do anything for you in pushing your book or obtaining you financial recognition I should be only too glad to do so.

*Sd./*W. M. P. WOOD.

(Copy of letter dated 2nd July, 1923, from Mr. J. T. Turner, Principal, Rajkumar College, and Member Bombay Provincial Scout Council).

To see what a trained man can do with an ordinary walking stick both in defence and attack is an eye-opener for the uninitiated. I have been privileged to watch a display given by men trained by Mr. H. G. Lang, Superintendent Agency Police, and was much impressed by the sight. It is difficult to realise what an extremely business–like weapon an ordinary walking stick can be without seeing it: I was much impressed and am convinced that all Boy Scouts should be taught to defend themselves in this way. The training involves physical exercises that are of great benefit in themselves, and teaches a boy to be quick on his feet and to keep cool in an emergency. I propose to introduce it as part of the training of Scouts here.

(Copy of letter dated 10th July, 1923, from Mr. T. F. Armstrong, A.M.I.A.E., F.R.S.A., Rajkot, Kathiawar).

I have had in the course of the last two years ample opportunity of forming an opinion on the use of a walking stick as a weapon of defence and offence from the numerous occasions I have witnessed the Kathiawar Agency Police at work with the stick. The surprising speed in its use acquired by practise, together with a knowledge of man's many vulnerable parts and the methods of employment under varying circumstances, *renders a walking stick into a weapon of the highest order for self-defence for the ordinary man in the street.* A very workable knowledge of how to employ a stick can be gathered from witnessing a demonstration and I have consequently, in view of the numerous opportunities I have had of doing so, the greatest faith in a walking stick if driven to employ it in self-defence.

(No. 485-B of 6th July, 1923. Subject: Instruction in stick drill).

Memorandum.

With a view to introducing the light stick in place of the lathi as a weapon of offence and defence in the hands of the Police, the Supdt. of Police (Nasik,★ Poona, Satara), is requested to send two of his best instructors to Rajkot for a month's instruction.

2. The actual date on which these men are to be sent should be arranged by direct correspondence with the Supdt. of Police, Kathiawar.

3. As the instructors now sent to Rajkot will be required to pass on their instruction not only to the men

★ Instructors have already been trained for several other districts in the Bombay Presidency and Sind.

at their own headquarters but also possibly to instructors of other districts, it is important that they should be first-class men.

4. The men will get daily allowance at the prescribed rate for the period of their halt while at Rajkot.

*Sd./*J. R. JACOB,
(for Inspector-General
of Police, Poona).

Chapter I

Introduction

Men no longer swagger abroad with swinging rapier and pistols thrust in the belt as they used in the golden days of old. We have become less picturesque, more matter-of-fact. But it is only an outward change. Our instinctive sense of self-preservation and self-protection still remains as it was.

Few men are seen nowadays without a stick of some kind in their hands while out; and what is a stick but the sign of an aesthetic progress whereby the prehistoric tree-limb has been whittled down to a bludgeon, the bludgeon to a club, to a walking stick, to an ornamental cane.

Times and manners change; and looking upon the walking stick as an adornment we are apt to overlook its origin and original use. We are sometimes brought to a rude sense of awakening by an unlooked for crisis, perhaps when confronted by a dangerous hooligan and his confraternity, a ferocious dog, a burglar. Attacks on individuals in railway carriages are also not of infrequent occurrence.

These contingencies, and many others, can be met, *by women as well as by men,* and very effectively met, when one has given back to the walking stick its primitively established use, and has acquired the knowledge of how to use it to its original purpose.

Boxing, Wrestling and Ju-Jitsu have taken the place of the stick. This is wrong! They should be scientific physical adjuncts and not substitutes. They are, unfortunately, not within the reach of all; and entail, if proficiency is the aim, a rigid carrying out of a strenuous course of instruction and training.

Our walking stick, our constant companion, the very feel of which is familiar, can be easily converted into a highly efficient means of self-defence with only a little amount of practice and no strenuous training. The peculiar advantage we then hold over the boxer, wrestler, and Ju-Jitsu exponent, will not fail to make itself apparent.

These, we will realize, may be overcome by even a very second rate opponent merely owing to the simple fact that they are not, except to a certain extent the last, provided with a means of meeting foul methods of attack. For example, a boxer is incapable of warding off a well-directed blow from a stick or a knife. His fist, arm, etc., most sensitive portions of his anatomy, as we will experience for ourselves, are easily vulnerable. The same holds good of the wrestler and to a certain extent the Ju-Jitsu exponent. They have *to get to grips* with their opponent before they can get to work, and therein lie their difficulty and danger; and this demonstrates our advantage over their methods in being able to deal with our opponent at a distance. This should not be taken as disparaging in any way these three most manly of sports which are of such vital importance in the training of the youth of the nation. Each is, in its way, an undoubted and highly efficient means of self-defence under certain circumstances, but, for the average man who is generally out of training, and has not the time or opportunity to get himself into training, a less strenuous and more decisive means of self-defence is afforded by a knowledge of how to employ a walking stick.

When you have attained proficiency with your stick you will realise that you are then in a position to deal with your opponents in the manner best suited to the circumstances. Lightly, if the situation is not serious, and with the utmost rigour should you be in any great peril.

By following the methods set forth in this book the average man *or woman* can quickly acquire proficiency. A casual glance through the book will enable the reader to grasp many hitherto unknown ways of converting a Walking Stick into a weapon of no mean order should the occasion to employ it arise.

On the Walking Stick as a weapon of defence for ladies, unescorted on rambles in the country, too much emphasis cannot be laid. Imagine the discomfiture of the burliest ruffian on sensing the deft manipulation of what appeared to him to be merely a harmless little Walking Stick.

For POLICE purposes, the methods described are invaluable. The average constable throughout the country is armed with that most unscientific weapon, the truncheon, too short to hit effectively with and too short to guard with. No scientific methods can be applied to its employment. It is up to the authorities to see that the men employed in the maintenance of law and order are instructed in a method of self-defence on scientific lines that can be employed by them under all circumstances and that will give them an advantage over those opposed to them. The introduction of these methods into the training of certain Police Forces in India has shown the readiness with which the men take to this form of training, and a knowledge of the methods tends, without a doubt, to the enhancement of the general efficiency of the whole force. The possibilities of a reduction in armaments of Police Forces, brought about by efficient training in these methods, are not to be discounted.

The scientific employment of a Walking Stick for purposes of self-defence will assuredly make a great appeal to all BOY

SCOUTS, and its inclusion in their training will afford a highly interesting and beneficial form of instruction that will go a long way toward engendering that very necessary spirit—self-confidence—which is so essential in all walks of life. We all aspire, or should aspire, to be expert in something, and surely the realisation that we are perfectly capable of looking after ourselves and of being able to render others a good turn in getting them out of a tight corner is worthy of achievement.

A certain BOY SCOUT troop in India has already realised the great benefits to be derived from training in the methods described in this book, and its introduction into their course of training has aroused the keenest desire in the boys to attain proficiency. It is possible that with them will lie the very great honour of introducing a change in the BOY SCOUT world by the substitution of the handy Walking Stick in place of the present unwieldy STAFF. Many actuated by motives of sentiment will possibly raise a protesting voice against any such change in the universally well-known BOY SCOUT kit, but in these days where there is only room for efficiency, which is after all the BOY SCOUTS' chief aim to attain, there will be nothing lost but a lot to be gained by the substitution of the Walking Stick for the STAFF for general use. The STAFF could be laid by for camp purposes if desired.

Perhaps the most potent consideration to be urged in favour of acquiring a knowledge of how to defend oneself with a stick is the feeling of security engendered by the knowledge that, given anything like a reasonable chance, one is able to render a very good account of oneself should the need arise.

The unfolding of the many ways of employing a stick which you have hitherto, perhaps, never really considered in this light, will prove of great interest and will act as a stimulus to continued effort to acquire proficiency in its use, besides which, in the performance of the numerous methods, you will have a form of exercise both beneficial and novel.

Certain of the exercises will occur to many as being somewhat brutal. This may be the case; but we must not overlook the fact that no sane person will employ them in any but the last resort. At the same time we should bear in mind that the individual who attacks us without provocation is unlikely to observe the "Don't hit below the belt" rule, and when up against such a one we owe it to ourselves and those dependent on us not to allow ourselves, in an affair not of our seeking, to be overcome by an opponent out to employ any means best suited to attain his own ends, "Your money or your life!"

In placing this book before the public the author feels confident that he will arouse no criticism on account of the language employed, and the absence of all attempt at style. He is out solely and only to place his methods before the public as simply as possible, without any attempt at effect. He has studiously subordinated flourishes to the straight line. His writing is the honest effort of a police officer in a distant and disturbed country to place before his fellow countrymen the concentrated result of long experience and experiment, in the hope that they will acquire proficiency in a less arduous way, and that each will learn to look upon his Walking Stick no less as a friend, but as a friend in the true sense of the word who will not fail at a time of emergency.

The work will appeal to all, more especially to those who have already been in a "tight corner" and have felt how much they missed in not having known how to use their stick to its best effect.

Do not forget: *we nearly all get into a "tight corner" some time or another, or are called upon to help others out.* Be ready; and the only way to get ready is to learn and then practise.

First of all you must dispel all ideas from the mind that such a light thing as a Walking Stick cannot be of much use, especially if your opponent is armed with a heavier stick or a knife, or if you are attacked by more than one at a time. It *can* be of much use. It will turn the scale in your favour. Have confidence. Keep an open mind on the subject until you have read through the book and practised the methods. Then you will be in a position to pronounce judgment.

YOUR WALKING STICK
HOW TO USE IT IN SELF-DEFENCE

BEST KIND OF STICK.

An ordinary Malacca Cane or an Ash Root Walking Stick (as in illustration Fig. 1) is the best. The latter has the advantage of being procurable for a few pence and will serve all requirements. The weight of the stick should be such as can be manipulated comfortably by the individual's wrist. Sacrifice weight to speed always, for remember that man is an easily vulnerable animal and has many soft spots—tap the back of your hand, inside of knee, shin, elbow, etc., etc., with your stick and experience for yourself. Once acquainted with the "Soft Spots" and the manner of getting at them, even the dandiest little cane will be converted into a by no means contemptible weapon of defence.

HOW TO HOLD STICK.

Grip stick about six inches up *thin* end; get a good balance; hold with thumb round stick—not resting on stick (Fig. 1). Maintain that grip always. At first the thumb will have a tendency to rest on the stick, but *do not allow it*. This tendency will be overcome after a little practise.

EXERCISES.

To employ your stick to its full advantage you must first go through the initial exercises; they all make for suppleness in wrist, shoulder, etc., and have the additional advantage of providing a beneficial and novel form of exercise in the performance of which you are accomplishing a double object, namely, doing your body a good turn and at the same time acquiring that necessary ease and rapidity of movement without which your stick play will be hampered. Get to know your stick. You can practise all these exercises while strolling along in the parks

FIG. I

or country. You can practise them at any odd moment until proficiency is yours, bearing in mind constantly the one great maxim in stick work without which all your efforts will be nullified. *Your stick hand must never drop below the level of your eyes.* The reason for this will be obvious to you as you progress, and will be pointed out later.

ON GUARD (Fig. 2).—Gripping stick as already described, bring right hand with straight arm well up and back over shoulder, stick sloping down with the point a little to left of and on level with eyes. The position of your body is the reverse of boxing. Right foot forward, body well balanced, weight on back leg. Left hand position is a matter of personal choice; it should be held so as to give the body the best poise and ready to be used as an additional guard. From this position practise all the subsequent exercises and perform them slowly at first.

EXERCISE 1.—Swing point of stick down to brush left hip and circle forwards and over shoulder; left hand tucked into side or extended to rear. You will see that when your point is down brushing left hip your hand will be near left side of head (above level of eyes!) and when your point is going forward your hand will also go with it to extreme arm length (hand above level of eyes!) Carry out this exercise until your stick swings round in rapid circles from the wrist, something after the style of a catherine wheel. This may be rather awkward to perform at first, but after a little practise you will quickly get into it. Do not forget to keep thumb round stick. This exercise is what is actually done when up against an opponent and within reach of him; one of your many little "Surprise Packets" so to speak. He will anticipate if anything a cut down at him—very well, give him a cut up!—his body, hand or chin

FIG. 2

is bound to be in the way. Never do what your opponent anticipates you are going to do! Subsequent methods will place you in possession of many such "Prize Packets." You may be in a tight corner with more than one opponent to be dealt with, so it behoves you to employ such decisive measures as will enable you to eliminate the number of your opponents as quickly as possible before their combined effort places you at a disadvantage.

EXERCISE 2.—Reverse the process. Swing point of stick down to brush left hip and circle upward (backwards), over the shoulder and forward (hand above level of eyes). As in the last exercise you will see that when your point is down brushing left hip your hand will be near left side of head (above level of eyes!) and when your point is going forward your hand will also go forward with it to extreme arm length. This movement exercises the exact method of tackling an opponent's head. Now, just to realise right away the effectiveness and handiness of your stick, suppose you have cut at opponent's head by this method and missed him, nothing is quicker than an employment of the "upper cut" method as shown in Exercise 1, for it is merely a manipulation of the wrist. This will make it more clear to you. Cut at an imaginary head by the method above described and without a fraction of a second's delay get into reverse along the same track (merely Exercise 1). You will see that like a flash your attack has shifted from the top of your opponent's head to his body, hand or chin whichever gets in the way first of your "Upper Cut." Even if you miss a real opponent he is most likely to be impressed by your effort! And a moral effect is already a tactical advantage. If your opponent is surprised it means he is off his guard and open to any other method you see your way to employ.

Practise these two exercises (as well as the subsequent ones) and, in fact, all; till you can do them speedily. The quicker you can make your stick revolve the better. Make it hum! If you find that the rapidity of movement causes a sensation of undue fatigue, then look to the poise of your stick or assure yourself as to its weight in relation to the strength of your wrist. *Err on light side always. It is speed you want, and not weight.*

Force and speed in delivering the cuts will come with practise. Your efforts at first will naturally lack force, but, in a short time, you will be able to deliver all cuts with surprising speed and force because it is largely a matter of wrist work.

EXERCISE 3.—Swing stick *parallel* to ground, right to left, so as just to brush top of head, hand working to and fro in front of face and above level of eyes. The hand goes to the front as point goes forward, and back towards forehead as the point goes to the rear. The hand should be nearly touching forehead when stick is pointing to the rear. Do not carry hand round head—*employ wrist* and keep hand working backwards and forwards only. Do not forget to have your stick parallel to the ground the whole time it is circling; the point will have a tendency to stick up in the air when going to the rear, but do not allow it and do not let your thumb wander. Perform all exercises slowly at first. You will drop into efficient performance of all exercises with surprising speed after a little practise.

You will appreciate this exercise later, for this is the method you will see is employed in all Cuts at left side of opponent, from face, neck, body, downwards.

EXERCISE 4.—Exactly the same as the Exercise we have just done only reverse the process. Swing stick the other way, left to right, and observe the same rules; stick must be parallel to ground and the hand working above level of eyes. This is the

FIG. 3

method you will soon see of delivering all Cuts on right of opponent's body, from face, neck, etc., downwards.

You will by now appreciate the fact that by these perform-ances you are above all things cultivating a supple wrist which is so essential for speed.

EXERCISE 5.—Perform Exercises 1 and 2 on right side of body. You have hitherto only done them on the left side.

EXERCISE 6.—Perform Exercises 1 and 2 alternately on both sides of body, first left, then right, very much after the style of Indian Club Swinging. Swing body in rhythm with the swing of your stick. See that stick brushes your hips and assure your-self that hand is *above level of eyes*. Be careful, too, that all instruc-tions as to performance of these exercises, as given above, are carried out. Practise as you swing along for your morning or evening walk in a quiet place where you can do no damage.

These exercises must be persisted in till they are smoothly carried out as if the joints were working in well-oiled bearings. Practise!

EXERCISE 7.—ARM AND SHOULDER EXERCISE. Stand to "Attention," hold stick in both hands, swing arms up full extent in line with body; and keeping arms extended, move them backward and forward above head smartly. The body must remain still (Fig. 3). This strengthens the muscles and quickly enables you to perform the exercises without any sense of effort.

CHAPTER III

GUARDS

Being peaceful men we shall first learn how to GUARD ourselves from attacks on our person, but to defend we must also attack! It would never do to assume a GUARD position and await the pleasure of our opponent to smite us with no fear of retaliation on our part. All GUARDS are therefore devised to give our opponent possibly more than he is capable of giving us. In fact, every guard we assume, in the very legitimate object of warding our person from danger, lays an opponent open to a very quick reply from us—a KNOCK OUT in a good many cases.

We shall first deal with the GUARDS pure and simple. Later on, and when the reader by dint of practise is in a position to appreciate it, we shall go on to the manner of taking advantage of these GUARDS by converting them into rapid and effective counters.

HEAD GUARD I.—FRONT GUARD: This you have already met with in the last chapter (Fig. 2) as a starting off position to enable you better to follow the exercises given. Assume position as described, right foot forward, toe straight to the front, body well balanced; weight on back leg. The left hand position is a matter of choice; it should be held so as to give the body the best poise, and, as you will see later, is a first class GUARD. The hand should be well back over shoulder, stick sloping with point of stick on side of face and about level with eyes. In this position the hand and head are safe, as a downward Cut from opponent will glance off your guard; and your hand, a SOFT SPOT, as you have already discovered, is far back out of danger. What would you do if attacked and your opponent had his hand within range of you? HIT IT! Eighty or more persons out of every hundred fail to realise that the hand is a very sensitive portion of their anatomy, and if damaged they are at the mercy of their opponent. Subsequent methods all tend to make you automatically get your hand out of danger. The guard position we are discussing is, of course, assumed only at the psychological moment to guard the head against a downward blow, and is employed against a weapon similar to our own. There are other methods for guarding against an opponent armed with a heavier weapon, but these will be dealt with in a succeeding chapter. The aim is to go on progressively and to perfect the knowledge already gained by constant practise.

HEAD GUARD 2.—CROSS GUARD: To appreciate these guards we will assume an opponent before us; this simplifies the description of the methods and enables us to appreciate the guards more fully. Let FRONT GUARD be your starting off position for all guards and in subsequent descriptions it will be assumed that you are in FRONT GUARD.

As your opponent's stick descends to head, swing your right hand over to left of head with an upward motion to meet opponent's descending stick; at the same time presenting your side to opponent. This gets you *under* your stick and adds force to your grip to resist descending blow. It is a very powerful guard. The stick must be tightly gripped. This is one of the many methods which will demonstrate clearly to you why your thumb should be round your stick and not resting on it. You would have no grip with your thumb on the stick. Have your hand high and clear of head with stick sloping backwards so

Fig. 4

that opponent's stick will glance off (Fig. 4). The harder the blow the quicker it is likely to glance off. Your reply to opponent from this position will be described to you in due course.

HEAD GUARD 3.—REAR GUARD (Fig. 5): As opponent's blow descends to head, withdraw right foot to rear smartly, maintaining your stick arm and stick in original position. Left hand, remember, is always comfortably held, and on the look out to get to work should an opportunity occur. This is a very efficient guard and in this position you have your opponent at a great disadvantage.

2.—BODY GUARD (left side): As opponent strikes at your face or body, swing body round from waist and bend body at waist towards the left by pulling in your left hip; at the same time drop your guard to meet blow, your right hand high, your stick gripped tight and forward of body, perpendicular to the ground. Your stick must be held forward of body so that if point of opponent's stick glances off your guard, your elbow, face or body will not be in danger. Tuck in left arm tight to side (Fig. 6). You can take a hard blow on your triceps if the elbow is tucked in tight without sustaining any damage. Again, your ribs are protected should your opponent get home. In this position you can open up like a spring trap to reply to your opponent.

3.—FLANK GUARD (right side): Drop point (lest you forget it is assumed you are in FRONT GUARD) and hold stick forward of body and perpendicular to ground. At the same time jerk your body round half-right from waist (Fig. 7). Another position for a very speedy reply to opponent.

4.—ANKLE AND LEG GUARD: As opponent strikes, do not drop HEAD GUARD; simply draw back right or left foot if you are in FRONT GUARD or REAR GUARD respectively (Fig. 8). Do it smartly, and get on to your toes ready to deliver your reply,

Fig. 5

Fig. 6

FIG. 7

FIG. 8

which should be like a flash after you have had a little practise and know how to do it.

5.—HAND AND WRIST GUARD: You may have tempted opponent to strike at your hand or *he* may know it is a "Soft Spot" and makes for it. Very well, shoot hand to rear smartly. You will be able to do this like a flash after practise and when sub-consciously you have fully realised the disadvantage of a smashed hand! On withdrawing hand to rear, throw shoulder back, keeping point of stick in front of and level with face (Fig. 9). Woe betide the unfortunate opponent if he has missed you!

FIG. 9

6.—GUARD AGAINST POINT (1): Do not forget the FRONT GUARD position you are assumed to be in. As opponent's point (stick, spear, whatever it is), comes in, drop point of your stick and, as your point drops, jerk body round from waist half-left smartly and pass opponent's point to your left side. You are then ready to reply to him (Figs. 10 and 11).

ANOTHER METHOD (2).—In the last chapter, Exercise 1, you circle upwards and forwards; very well, to guard against point, instead of circling your stick as in Exercise 1, circle your stick *across* your front. Hand above level of eyes. Make the stick hum;

FIG. 10

FIG. 11

the hum will develop with practise. No point can get in at you as long as you keep your stick circling. Opponent in attempting futile thrusts will lay himself open to the employment of one of the many methods you will have at your disposal.

Practise these guards assiduously. Perfection will come with constant repetition, and with perfection rapidity of movement.

Chapter IV

Cuts

We now pass on to the various methods of delivering Cuts, and this is where you will appreciate the Exercises laid down in Chapter II, for they have all been devised with a definite object in view, as will be now demonstrated to you.

Head Cut (1).—*Never* strike at opponent's head as in illustration (Fig. 12) for, as you will see, he may save himself even if his stick is just above the level of his head. Always deliver a head cut with hand as high as possible (Fig. 13). Exercise 2 in the first chapter now comes to your aid in showing how a cut at your opponent's head should be delivered. From your Front Guard position, which has been already explained to you, swing point of your stick downwards to brush left hip in circuitous motion to the rear, cut finishing up with hand high and arm fully extended, palm of hand up, body sideways and raised on toes. The point of your stick will finish up below level of your hand, stick sloping down with every chance of point getting home over your opponent's guard. The value of a high guard is obvious, hence the necessity for a straight arm in your Head Guards (1) and (3). In passing, just refer to Fig. 14 and see what a very effective means you have of employing two cuts should your cut at head fail to have reached. Merely a turn of the wrist and your stick travels backwards over the course it came, to opponent's body, hand or chin. This you will

Fig. 12

FIG. 13

be able to accomplish like a flash after a little practise—all wrist work—hence the speed.

FACE OR NECK CUT.—This is where Exercises 3 and 4 come in. They prepare you for the motion you will have to perform in delivering all Cuts either on the left or right side of your opponent.

CUT LEFT.—Get into FRONT GUARD position. From your FRONT GUARD, carry out the instructions in Exercise 3. Cut, with stick parallel to ground, right to left. Your stick should be held so as just to brush head. *Cut with the wrist,* keeping hand as

Fig. 14

far as possible in front of face and above level of eyes. The tendency at first will be to carry hand all round head, which means that the wrist is not being fully employed, but you will soon get the "Knack" if you carry out the initial Exercise 3. Let your Cut be of a glancing nature and finish up in FRONT GUARD position. Your stick should slide off opponent's body, face, etc., in the original direction of the Cut, back on its way to guard your head. In all such Cuts your stick completes a circle. No time is therefore lost in getting on to guard again. In other words, do not let your stick stop on opponent's body or his guard, if he has one; let it glance off in its original direction back on to ON GUARD.

You are here learning how to look after two very vulnerable parts, the head and the hand. As has already been stated, you will in time automatically cover them the moment they have been exposed while delivering a Cut, etc. After every Cut cover your head and hand by getting into HEAD GUARD either FRONT GUARD or REAR GUARD, for your opponent may try to give you a quick reply. You must take no risks!

BODY CUT, KNEE CUT, SHIN CUT.—Exactly the same as above only drop to the level of the part you are cutting at (Figs. 15 and 16). Do not forget the glancing cut and back on to guard like a flash after every cut. Always cut inwards at knee or shin for the inside is less protected than the outside, and drop level with your cut. By dropping, the head is always under cover of a speedy guard. This is not the case if you stand up and cut low at opponent for your hand is taken a long distance from your head, and recovering of head is therefore much less speedy. You will now realise the necessity for the emphasis laid on the fact that, as far as possible, *hand must be above level of eyes in delivering cuts,* so that it only has a little way to go back when you have to protect it and your head with a HEAD GUARD. Keep your hand as near home as you possibly can!

CUT RIGHT.—We will now consider cuts on the right side of your opponent's person. They are delivered in exactly the same way as cuts on his left side; but, at first, you will find this rather more difficult to perform because there is just a little "Preparation" required in commencing this cut which you do not experience in the more straightforward cut at his left side. It is well worth cultivating and will always be a surprise to the ordinary man when it comes in. Not to you, of course, because you have your FLANK GUARD to meet it! Practise this CUT RIGHT slowly at first. From FRONT GUARD position let your stick circle to the right, round your head (this is the

FIG. 15

"Preparation") and your hand acting as a pivot. When your stick point is coming to the front on the left side of your head, extend your arm, viz., reach out to get at opponent wherever you want to hit him—face, neck, body, etc. Like everything else speed will come with practise and force with it. Do not forget the glancing blow and back on to FRONT GUARD like a flash. Your stick will have performed a circle round your head. Practise cuts at different portions of your opponent's body in turn—imagining a post, tree, or anything as your opponent.

Scientific reasons for Glancing Cut:—

1. There is very much more shock behind it than behind a dead blow. A glancing or wiping cut on neck will sever the jugular vein.

Fig. 16

2. Stick in delivering cut is on its way back to guard the head without a pause.

3. There is every chance of getting in on opponent after glancing off his guard; either getting in on face, side, or elbow, and there is also every chance of being able to employ a "Flick," to which you will soon be introduced.

4. A stick delivering a dead blow can be caught by an opponent—this is another reason why you are instructed to keep your hand ready for employment when an opportunity to employ it should arise. If a glancing blow is caught, do not forget there is a *pull* behind a glancing blow and none in a dead one, and the chances of a grip being maintained are slight. *A cut with the wrist is always a glancing cut.*

How to Deliver Point—From Front Guard position jab down into opponent's face or chest. Let the point make contact with a jab with weight behind it. Do not withdraw hand before delivering a point. Never give an indication to opponent of what you intend doing.

Chapter V

Combination of Cut and Guard

You are now approaching a stage where you might be initiated into the rather more complex combination of cuts and guards. So far we have combined all cuts with FRONT GUARD in which without exception we finish up—the reason has already been explained (to protect head and hand). We now go a step further and combine our cuts with our CROSS GUARD (Chapter 2, Fig. 4) and we shall now see how this is employed.

ON GUARD.—Get into FRONT GUARD as imaginary opponent strikes at you, or you may ask your friend to do so, but deal lightly with him! Get into CROSS GUARD, as described, by swinging your hand over to left of head with an upward tendency, body sideways, stick well sloping back and hand away from head out of danger. Descending blow will glance off stick, and opponent will be exposed to an immediate reply to his head, face or neck by a turn of your wrist (Figs. 17, 18). To add force to blow swing your whole body to right at the same time as you cut. This is a terrific cut so it is advisable to practise on an imaginary opponent!

We shall now carry this combination a bit further by supposing you have *two* opponents to deal with. Both are rushing in at you and time is precious. Take No. 1, the nearest one to you, with a CUT LEFT as you now know how to carry out, and instead of wasting precious time in getting into FRONT GUARD,

FIG. 17

finish up your cut in CROSS GUARD, and reply from there to No. 2. This is a very useful method, for No. 2 may be directing a blow at your head and your GUARD is there ready to receive it before replying (Fig. 19). Now supposing that your opponents are on you and you judge that there is no time to employ your CROSS GUARD after you have dealt with opponent No. 1.

FIG. 18

Very well, employ *two* CUTS LEFT, one for each opponent, in quick succession without coming into any guard in between. After completing your second cut, get into CROSS GUARD and travel back along the same track with your terrific cut, and if they are still in the way they will catch it. You are thereby making doubly sure of getting in some cut or other.

This is the method to practise what we have just discussed.

FORMING SQUARE.—Give it a name! Imagine you are attacked. Carry out two continuous sharp cuts—CUT LEFT— one in front of you, the second half left. Finish up your second cut in CROSS GUARD. Now imagine an opponent on the right still remaining to be dealt with. Cut right from CROSS GUARD and swinging body round with cut, let your right arm go out to fullest extent with your cut. Repeat same cuts until you have completed a circle. Let your body swing round with your cut to right from CROSS GUARD. This is excellent practise and

Fig. 19

makes for free and easy play with your stick. Do not forget to *employ your wrist* with your cuts. Practise delivering three cuts in quick succession, finishing up in CROSS GUARD and then CUT RIGHT from your CROSS GUARD position. Do not forget to employ the wrist and glancing blow. Make your stick buzz round—it is surprising the pace you can get into your cuts.

You will by now be realising your formidable proportions so you will be taken a step still further and shown something else which makes for free and easy play with your stick, and may be decidedly useful if you are cramped for space such as in a room, railway carriage, mob, or even in the street, to deal with a single opponent who is too close to you to be dealt with otherwise.

We will call this CLEARING PRACTISE. ON GUARD (FRONT GUARD). Cut down at opponent's body (as already pointed out: we adopt a start being made from FRONT GUARD to simplify understanding of the method). Let your cut finish up in rear of body, stick parallel to ground and under left arm (Fig. 20). Your body has swung round with the force of your cut. Left arm up ready for use. From this position swing your body round from waist and let your cut be of a glancing nature, finishing up parallel to ground and under level of shoulder, elbow close to side (Fig. 21). Crouch to it. From this position swing body left from waist back into first position (Fig. 20). Back again once more to position (Fig. 21). You have now completed four cuts at opponent's body. Perform practise slowly at first. Increase speed gradually. After a little practise you will be able to go through the four cuts without a pause between the cuts, and there will be an unbroken hum of the stick throughout the four cuts. Get your shoulder round with a jerk. No wrist work comes in here. *Your shoulder is the motive power.* These are very powerful cuts. You will appreciate this method for close quarter work if you stand in a doorway and see how your cuts take effect on the sides of the doorway. Let there be a pull behind your cuts and bring the shoulder round with a jerk. Crouch to it. To appreciate this method of cutting more fully, stand close to a person with your hand about level with your waist and *slowly* revolve right, with your stick parallel to ground; you will realise you hit him in the middle, a tender spot, and you can appreciate the effect your blow would have if you jerked round your shoulder in real earnest.

Do not forget, cut to left finishing up below left arm, stick parallel to ground, and cut to right finishing up below level of

FIG. 20

FIG. 21

shoulder. Make your stick hum and get a pull behind it. Do not flick stick round with wrist otherwise it won't come round in a tight place. Pull it round with your shoulder.

Practise this method also on the move. You may have to cut your way out of a mob. Cut to left as the right foot advances so as to get the whole swing of the body behind the blow. Cut to right as the left foot advances and so on with a rhythmical swing of the body. It all makes for free and easy play with your stick. Practise! You will then be able to form an estimate of the efficiency of your stick when it is properly handled.

CHAPTER VI

EVERY GUARD
LAYS AN OPPONENT OPEN
TO A QUICK REPLY

You will now be able to appreciate the efficiency of your guards and the position in which they place you to the disadvantage of your opponent. You have already seen in the last chapter what a very speedy reply you are able to give opponent from your CROSS GUARD position. We will now consider the other guards in turn.

REAR GUARD.—Do not forget in REAR GUARD that you have your left foot forward. Having guarded opponent's blow at head, his stick will slide down your sloping guard (Fig. 22). Reply at once with a twist of your wrist to left; it is merely a CUT LEFT to his face, neck, etc. (Fig. 23). Do not forget, a glancing blow, and then back on to ON GUARD.

BODY GUARD (Fig. 6).—You are a veritable spring trap in this position, and there are no fewer than three methods of taking advantage of opponent, after you have guarded his blow.

(1) Open up! Throw left arm to rear and deliver simultaneous HEAD CUT (1), a turn of the wrist, that is all.

(2) Open up! and deliver the UPPER CUT from your guard position. Let your stick flick straight up to chin or body, and employ the left arm to add force to your cut by shooting it back.

FIG. 22

(3) Grip your stick with left hand, lower point and jump at opponent's throat, face, etc.

FLANK GUARD (Fig. 7).—Exactly the same replies as from BODY GUARD; swing stick to brush left hip for the HEAD CUT and flick up stick from wrist for the UPPER CUT, left hand is ready to be employed.

When delivering all cuts at head, reach up as high as possible to get in over guard of opponent (Fig. 13).

HAND OR WRIST GUARD (Fig. 9).—Withdraw hand as you have been shown how to do; and from the far back position you have assumed you are able instantly to thrust forward point of stick to opponent's face, etc., or to deliver a "Flick" which we are soon coming to.

LEG, SHIN, OR ANKLE GUARD (Figs. 8 and 24).—Withdraw foot smartly to avoid opponent's blow (if opponent has a long stick, spring back, finishing up on your toes, with both feet together—you can spring back with ease a couple of yards), get on your toes, and swinging point of stick to brush left hip, lunge out again with foot which was withdrawn and deliver cut on opponent's head, etc. (Fig. 25). Failing this, see Fig. 14.

You may have taken a fancy to the CROSS GUARD, and would like to employ it whenever possible to guard your head.

FIG. 23

Fig. 24

FIG. 25

Now, if you are in FRONT GUARD you can easily do so, but in REAR GUARD (left foot forward) you will have to alter the position of your feet, otherwise you cannot get into CROSS GUARD. If you did, you would be all tied up in a very uncomfortable position, and the guard would not be efficient. This is the way to get into CROSS GUARD from REAR GUARD: As opponent's stick descends, bring your right foot forward in a lunge; keep low, and at the same time shoot up your stick hand to left of head, body sideways to opponent, stick well sloping.

All the guards have their advantages, so practise them all.

Replies to opponents from guard positions should be very speedy, and it is only a matter of getting familiar with the handling of your stick.

Chapter VII

"Flicks" and "Flips"

We are now beginning to go ahead in real earnest and we shall soon reach the ACTIVE PLAY stage where we shall be employing our feet for quick work. Up to the present we have been going through the methods in a more or less fixed position except in the FORMING SQUARE practise and CLEARING PRACTISE on the move. We are gradually getting a "Grand Combination" of methods together, from which we will be able to choose according to the circumstances under which we are placed in defending ourselves.

Certain new methods hitherto merely referred to, will now be introduced.

THE FLICK.—"Flicks" are most effective when properly delivered. They are capable of being very speedily delivered and are very difficult to guard as they curve round and get in behind a guard, though the guard may be perfect against a cut.

HOW TO DELIVER A "FLICK."

As before, start from FRONT GUARD. (You will later on see that a FLICK can be delivered from any position). From your FRONT GUARD lead straight into your imaginary opponent's face as in delivering a "Point." Aim at the part you want to

Fig. 26

strike. Shoot the arm out to its fullest extent, and with a turn of the wrist to the left, make contact (Fig. 26).

Practise delivering the Flick slowly at first and put your whole body into it; shooting left arm to rear as right goes forward and hollowing the back when the wrist is turned. *Always deliver the* Flick *with a lunge.*

A Flick may be likened to the crack of a whip. The turn of the wrist makes the crack, as it were. This method of employing your stick should be persisted in till proficiency is reached. It is a highly efficient method of employing a stick in self-defence. When you realise that a Flick, properly delivered, will splinter a piece of wood a quarter of an inch thick, the effect on an opponent can be imagined!

In a tight corner a FLICK is particularly useful. What a very useful method for a railway carriage or any tight corner with your back to a wall where you cannot employ your cuts?

For preference, practise on a board nailed to a tree or post, or an old outhouse door. The resounding "Smack" encourages one to effort until the stage is reached when the resounding, clean and finished "Smack" resembles more the deft kick of a

FIG. 27

racehorse on a stable door, rather than the laboured clumsy effort of a carthorse at the same game. A kick from a racehorse will drop you, whereas a carthorse will lift you into the next field, and you may still get up smiling! It is all a matter of finish, so cultivate the racehorse finish in your "Flick."

Another rather similar stroke is the FLIP. Also a very efficient way of employing your stick under all circumstances when attacked. To deliver a FLIP: from any position spring at your opponent, with point of stick straight for face or body, and judging your distance so as to reach opponent with fully extended arm. Make contact by jerking wrist up (Fig. 27). This is different from the FLICK in that the jerk of the wrist is upwards, whereas in the FLIP, the turn of the wrist is to the left. A FLIP is very difficult to guard. You will see this if you imagine an opponent in front of you and you make for his face. If his guard is formed to cover his head you will come under it on to his face; and if he tries to guard his face you can come in on his head. After delivering a FLIP spring back again for a repetition if necessary or to be ready for emergencies. Practise FLIPS in a similar way to FLICKS; both well deserve special consideration and high development as they are potent arguments to urge in getting out of a tight corner, more especially, when time is not on your side and your opponents require to be quickly convinced.

The surprising speed with which FLICKS and FLIPS can be delivered after a little practise, will develop you into a veritable automatic "Flick—Flip—Repeater," automatic feed, no reloading! "Some Gun," remarks our Yankee friend!

Chapter VIII

Active Stick Play

Our old friend Exercise 1 in the first chapter of this book has not been referred to for a long time; this is where he comes in. He is well worth cultivating.

When confronted by an opponent never stand still in front of him. If he looks like business and is formidable, get down into CIRCLING GUARD like a shot, right foot forward. Exercise 1 will henceforth be known as CIRCLING GUARD. Make your stick hum round in UPPER CUTS as you will by now know how to do. This will in all probability upset the calculations of your opponent and will, if your first few upper cuts miss him, certainly make him stagger back and be at a disadvantage. Do not forget that the moral effect of a stick, "whizzing" in front of an opponent with every chance of getting home, is extremely disconcerting to him! When employing your CIRCLING GUARD you will naturally judge your distance so as to get home straight away. You do not want to show your opponent what you are going to do. It does not matter if your initial move by the first upper cut misses. Follow your opponent up or retire (still circling your stick) as the case may be. Make use of your feet; short, sharp, active steps, forwards or backwards, like the boxer.

From your CIRCLING GUARD on the move, either backwards or forwards, practise all GUARDS and CUTS which have been already described to you. Before we proceed any further, remember one thing, and that is, *in getting into any guard always step in towards opponent.* The nearer you are to him the less chance you stand of being· hurt, for you lessen the force of opponent's cut. This you will have very clearly demonstrated to you in a subsequent chapter.

Again, you must remember that when employing your CIRCLING GUARD, your stick should never cease circling until the psychological moment arrives of getting into a guard or of delivering a cut.

Practise getting into FRONT GUARD from CIRCLING GUARD. Up goes your hand to its old refuge, straight arm, well back over shoulder, head and hand safe should opponent have managed to deliver blow at head. The same with CROSS GUARD; from CIRCLING GUARD, whip up your hand to left of head into CROSS GUARD. Practise this until you can get off CIRCLING GUARD into any other guard like a flash; you will find that your other guards are formed simultaneously with the stoppage of your CIRCLING GUARD. From your CIRCLING GUARD practise all cuts; let your CIRCLING GUARD run into the cuts as it were. There should be no stoppage between your CIRCLING GUARD and your CUTS. After delivering a cut get into the habit of immediately covering your head. ON GUARD at once (i.e., HEAD GUARD). Since the head and hand are vital spots it is obviously necessary to acquire the habit of immediately recovering them every time they have been exposed in delivering a cut; for opponent may have guarded your cut and give a reply. Take no risks! If he does not give a reply you can get down into your CIRCLING GUARD again, if necessary. The great point is you can change from your CIRCLING GUARD into any other guard or cut like a flash, after practise. The change will be automatic.

Get down into your CLEARING PRACTISE from your CIRCLING GUARD, deliver the four cuts as you have been taught how to do, then back into CIRCLING GUARD again. This is splendid practise for free and easy play with your stick. From your CIRCLING GUARD, your stick humming round, do not forget, practise FLICKS and FLIPS as before, no stop; a continuous movement straight from CIRCLING GUARD into a FLICK or FLIP. Practise slowly at first till you get into it.

TO DELIVER A FLICK OR FLIP FROM CIRCLING GUARD.—As your stick revolves and point goes to the front, lunge out for your FLICK or FLIP.

You will soon get into it and you will realise what an extraordinarily efficient weapon of self-defence you will have converted your hitherto useless Walking Stick into.

Now that we have arrived at this stage, the use of the left hand and arm as a GUARD will be demonstrated to you. We have so far only referred to the left hand and arm for employment in adding force to CUTS, FLICKS AND FLIPS, for seizing opponent's stick or other weapon should it come within reach, and also for giving poise to the body. We will now see how the left arm can be employed as a guard.

The left arm is a very efficient secondary guard, and the hardest blow at the head can be guarded by shooting the left arm up to meet the descending blow. As the blow descends shoot the left arm up to its fullest extent to meet the blow. The fingers should be closed, the hand in its upward flight describing a spiral motion, finishing with fully extended arm and palm turned to the left with a jerk. A blow will glance off without any injury to arm (Fig. 28). Arm must be shot straight up like a flash, for it would not do for descending blow to land on a bent arm when it would not glance off without damage. It is all a matter of practise. Do not forget, the fingers *closed,* the spiral motion of hand, and the very necessary finish with a jerk of the palm of hand to the left. The employment of the left arm as a guard for a blow delivered at your body will be described in the next chapter in a method for disarming an opponent.

FIG. 28

Chapter IX

Trick Methods

We now come on to some very interesting methods of employing our stick in self-defence and we shall all like them, because they are so simple and require such a little expenditure of effort to carry them out. In getting acquainted with them you must, however, not lose sight of our old friends, the GUARDS, CUTS, FLICKS, FLIPS, etc., because they can be so very useful on occasions and may see you out of many a tight corner.

TRICK 1.—Feint at opponent's head (Fig. 29). Let the feint be slow and obviously as if you intended delivering a cut at head. Opponent will certainly try to guard the blow, and as his guard goes up jerk back your stick; merely a turn of your wrist; get into reverse in other words; grip your stick with the left hand also and jump in to deliver. JAB in throat or stomach (Fig. 30). Keep your elbows tucked into side and point of your stick up. The JAB has the whole weight of your body behind it.

After practise you will see that you get in like a flash, for you will be jumping forward at the same time as your stick is dropping to your left hand. Stick should be grasped with knuckles of left hand up.

TRICK 2.—Instead of jumping in as in the above Trick, grasp your stick as it comes back into the left hand and lunge for stomach with fully extended left arm (Fig. 31). Speed is developed with practise.

Fig. 29

Trick 3.—Feint at opponent's head in the same way, with your Head Cut. You must bear in mind that in all feints, your opponent must be led to believe that you intend delivering a cut at the point you first make for, your object being to get his guard away from the part you wish to smite. Having feinted, you make a clean sweep from head to knee of opponent: all carried through without a pause. Drop with your cut. Cover head and hand after cut. Do not forget to do so.

Trick 4.—Reverse of No. 3 above. Drop as if about to deliver a cut at opponent's knee, down will come his guard. Then, without a pause sweep stick up to opponent's head.

Fig. 30

FIG. 31

FIG. 32

FIG. 33

Finish up all head cuts, do not forget, with hand as high as possible (Fig. 13).

TRICK 5.—Feint with a CUT LEFT at opponent's face (Fig. 32) and without coming into contact with his guard, draw back stick and in one continuous movement shove out arm to its fullest extent for a FLICK on face (Fig. 33).

TRICK 6.—As opponent's stick descends toward head "slip" left; merely a short, sharp, side step, in order to get out of the way of his stick. As you side step, cut at his knees. Let your cut be like a flash, for in cutting, your arm has to pass under opponent's descending stick. If you miss his knee, grasp stick with left hand, elbows well into side, and jump in to deliver JAB in face, neck, armpit, or ribs. Side step and jump forward without a pause (Fig. 34). If opponent at the time of striking has his left

Fig. 34

foot forward he will, if you miss his knee, receive JAB in throat or chest. Appreciate the fact that the whole weight of your body is behind the JAB.

TRICK 7.—If circumstances are such that you do not want unduly to damage your opponent (though he strikes at you as in Trick 6 above, and has his right leg forward), step left as his blow descends towards head, and, in jumping in at him, thrust your stick high up between his thighs and at the same time give a sharp push

F<small>IG</small>. 35

away to right. Your opponent is violently spun round and thrown, and at your mercy to deal with by other methods according to circumstances (Fig. 35). You need not wait for him to strike at you to employ this and the subsequent Trick method. If he looks like business, down him! It will possibly save any exchange of blows.

T<small>RICK</small> 8.—The same as above trick only opponent is standing with his left leg forward. As blow descends to head, jump smartly in to his left, thrust stick in between his thighs and push

FIG. 36

left with a jerk (Fig. 36). This spins him round violently and it is your fault if he gets the better of you.

TRICK 9—A great principle is introduced here and one which will be at all times invaluable to you. It is:—

THE NEARER YOU ARE TO AN OPPONENT THE LESS CHANCE YOU STAND OF BEING HURT IF HE IS STRIKING AT YOU.

The real "business end" of a stick is the last foot or so, and the further up the stick you go, the lesser becomes the danger. The

FIG. 37

following method, which we shall call DISARMING PRACTISE, will clearly demonstrate this to you. Supposing you have an opponent before you, and you wish to employ this method. Very well, get into REAR GUARD (do not forget your left leg forward). Watch your opportunity, and judge your distance by employing foot play. As opponent strikes at head, face or body, jump in, left leg forward, at the same time shooting left arm out fully extended as already explained at the end of the last chapter. Let left arm come round in a swinging left "hook" so that opponent's hand or stick is caught high up in your armpit. Keep right arm high, and, as you deliver hook with left arm, rise on your toes and arch your back. Keep your right arm straight up in guard position when jumping in, for, if your right arm is down, your elbow will be in danger from opponent's stick circling round body when it is suddenly arrested by your grip under armpit. When jumping in, merely carry point of your stick to the front by a turn of the wrist, keeping a straight arm ready to drive home into opponent's face or neck. JAB to face or neck is delivered simultaneously with "hook" by left arm (Fig. 37).

It will be observed that, instead of driving point of stick into opponent's face or neck, his elbow can be severely damaged by swinging point of stick down with a turn of the wrist (Fig. 38).

DISARMING PRACTISE is well worth cultivating. Practise at first with someone cutting at your body. You will see that if you do not go in, you are liable to be hurt; whereas, the further up your opponent's stick you go, the danger will be proportionately lessened until you reach his hand, where he cannot possibly hurt you. In actual practise you will find that you secure opponent's hand in a vice-like grip in your armpit, and by rising on your toes, you are liable to severely damage his wrist. By this method, if an opponent is hitting hard, his stick actually flies out of his hand. Practise taking cuts at your head in exactly the same way as the BODY CUT. Opponent's hand is brought neatly to rest under your arm by your swinging left "hook."

TRICK 10.—Having deposited your opponent on the ground by certain of the above trick methods, you may desire to keep him there. This is a very simple matter. Plant the point of your stick in the pit of his stomach and lean lightly on your stick. This is dangerous, as too much pressure might be fatal. You are quite safe as he is incapable of moving (Fig. 39).

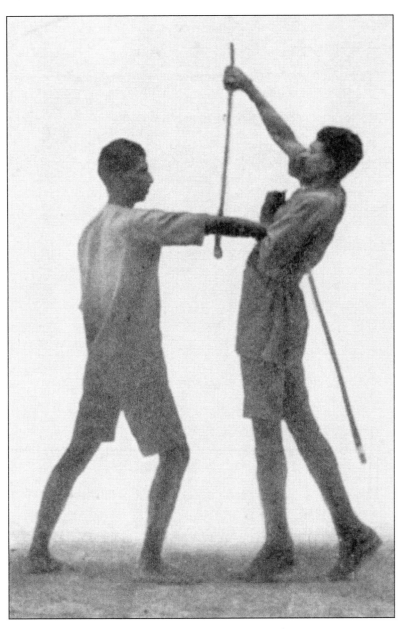

FIG. 38

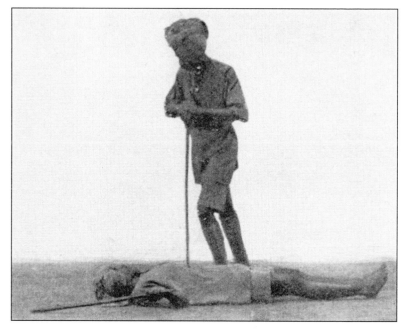

FIG. 39

TRICK 11.—Supposing you are disarmed or have been attacked suddenly when empty handed; the following method will be of great service, in addition to the method described to you in TRICK 9, for you now realise that you can tackle an opponent empty-handed by your DISARMING PRACTISE method in just the same way as if you had a stick in your hand. Employ your fist in place of the point of your stick.

Wait for your opponent to strike. Judge your distance and make use of the foot play you have been taught. As opponent's stick descends to head, jump in, left leg forward, as in DISARMING PRACTISE; carry left forearm across and forward of face so as to receive opponent's forearm on it.

FIG. 40

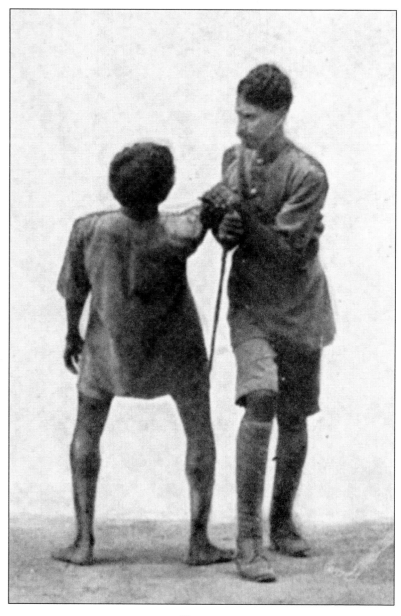

Fig. 41

F<small>IG</small>. 42

At the same time bring the back of your right hand up with a smack against his triceps. This bends his arm at the elbow (Fig. 40). Lock your hands and drop your left elbow, carry your right leg forward and throw opponent (Fig. 41); maintaining same hold on reaching the ground, and plant your knee in his armpit. He can then be held with the right hand only (Fig. 42). The method is illustrated in stages to demonstrate it more clearly; the whole being, of course, one motion without a stop. Practise this with a friend who realises he is expected to fall back and not to offer any resistance. Let him hit as hard as he likes, but after that, give in and go back. In actual practise opponent's stick will fly out of his hand when his downward blow is arrested by your forearm, and he will have a very badly damaged shoulder by the time you get him to the ground.

Before we close this chapter you should remember that, should you judge yourself unable at the last moment to carry out a particular trick, you have always your old friends the numerous guards to fall back on to protect yourself against the impending blow.

Chapter X

Double Handed Stick Play

You will find the following methods extremely useful if you are up against an opponent armed with a heavy stick, staff, or cudgel. They are extremely easy to grasp at this stage for you have already acquired a knowledge of how to guard yourself and to deliver cuts; and you will easily outclass an opponent with heavy armament. You will sail round him like a light craft, for his movements will necessarily be impeded by his unwieldy weapon. The first method of dealing with him you will now realise after the care you have taken of acquiring the knack of guarding your own hand. It should be a cut at his hand, a FLICK, a FLIP, CUTS, UPPER CUT with your CIRCLING GUARD, or the numerous tricks learnt in the last chapter. However, here are further methods of dealing with him.

ON GUARD (Fig. 43).—Get into your FRONT GUARD position and grasp stick with both hands behind shoulder ready for attack, and do not forget your foot play, backwards and forwards, as the case may be. From this position your opponent has no indication from which direction your attack will be launched. In fact, it is extremely unlikely he will be in a hurry to attack you, as he will scent danger. However, if he risks a blow at your head you are ready.

HEAD GUARD.—Jump in as blow descends (you must step in for all guards, do not forget) and let your arms arrive at fullest

FIG. 43

FIG. 44

extent with a jerk, taking opponent's *hands* on your stick (Fig. 44). The result will be his stick flies over your head and he sustains a badly damaged hand; for if he is striking at you at all he will naturally put force into his blow.

If he strikes at the left side of your body, your old friend the BODY GUARD comes in, only this time a double-handed one (Fig. 45); and how to reply you already know. It is quite simple; release the left hand for your HEAD CUT and UPPER CUT or jump in straight away with your stick grasped in both hands for a JAB in face, neck, etc., which you know well how to do by now. There is nothing to prevent you using your DISARMING PRACTISE methods; merely release the left hand as you jump forward for your swinging left "hook."

FLANK GUARD.—If opponent strikes at your right side, employ a double handed FLANK GUARD (Fig. 46), and reply as you already know how to do. In coming into all double-handed guards, maintain the grip with both hands on your stick, *and see that your right hand is always uppermost in* BODY *and* FLANK GUARDS, so that your replies are not impeded as they would be if your left hand was uppermost. There is nothing new in these guards or counters. They are only a varied form of what you have already learnt.

CUTS.—Do not give opponent any indication from which direction he may expect your CUTS.

CUT LEFT.—Simultaneously with the release of the stick by your left hand lunge out with the right leg. This jerks shoulder round to add speed and force to the CUT (Fig. 47). All should be done in one movement; the CUT is delivered like a flash, and you get straight back on to ON GUARD.

CUT RIGHT (Fig. 48).—Exactly the same, except that the right hand is released, and you lunge forward with left leg and deliver CUT. ON GUARD!

FIG. 45

FIG. 46

FIG. 47

FIG. 48

FIG. 49

FIG. 50

FIG. 51

CUT UP ON RIGHT (Fig. 49).—This is where Exercises 5 and 6, which we have left so very far behind, come to our aid, though we may not have appreciated their true value at the time we performed them. They give us a supple shoulder and wrist, and are therefore worth going through as we stroll along for a walk. Exactly the same procedure; simultaneous release of stick by left hand with lunge by right leg and sweeping upper cut from a supple shoulder and wrist.

UPPER CUT ON LEFT (Fig. 50).—This now needs no description after what has been said.

Herewith yet another method of dealing with your opponent. As his stick descends toward your head, step smartly to the right and swing round left to deliver cut across wrist or hand of opponent (Fig. 51).

By this stage it is well ingrained into you how to protect your hand so that when employing these methods you can be left to see, when receiving a blow on your guard, that neither hand is in the way of the blow.

You already know how to guard your legs and you have appreciated the great advantage of jumping into an opponent to lessen the force of his blow. You may now safely be left to do so.

CHAPTER XI

HOW TO DEAL WITH AN OPPONENT UNDER SPECIAL CIRCUMSTANCES

So far we have presumed our opponent to be armed with a stick or cudgel, the weapon he is most likely to employ. Having now at your disposal a whole battery of methods to bring to your aid in self-defence, you can realise that, provided you are given warning, an opponent armed, for instance, with a knife, would be at the mercy of your powerful UPPER CUTS, HEAD CUTS, etc., FLICKS, FLIPS, and the host of other methods you have now acquired a knowledge of. The odds would be all on your side. Similarly, the gentleman who draws a revolver within reach of you could also be very speedily despatched before he realised what you were about.

Take the case of an opponent rushing in at you who has arrived too close before you are able to employ your more open methods. Grasping the stick in both hands, as in Fig. 30, you can receive him with the point of your stick at his throat or get down to the employment of your CLEARING PRACTISE method.

You may be driven to take up your stand with your back to a wall. In this position you are deprived of the employment of your cuts, as your stick cannot go back. Here you will appreciate your FLICKS and FLIPS above all other methods. Should you find yourself in such a position lunge out at your nearest opponents with a FLICK or FLIP; this enables you to leave your cramped position against the wall, and you can get in your cuts and guards in rapid succession as you did in the chapter on ACTIVE STICK PLAY, before you again get your back to the wall for protection to await another opportunity for a sally forward. A knowledge of how to act under such circumstances does at least afford one a fighting chance of coming out of a tight corner.

If driven to employ your stick in self-defence in a mob, room, railway carriage or similar tight corner where you have not much elbow room, get down into the CLEARING PRACTISE method and use your shoulder as you have been told how to do. From this position your FLICKS and FLIPS can be very speedily delivered all round you, if you make active use of your feet. Very effective play can be made by grasping stick in both hands, and jabbing upwards with both ends, left and right, using the shoulder to its best advantage. The moral effect of one or two FLICKS or FLIPS, well delivered, is considerable, and may make a mob get back from you to think, and your chance of escape lies in seizing such an opportunity.

The SAND BAGGER or other opponent attacking from behind, can, if his approach is heard, be met by a swinging cut to the rear as you face about by the CLEARING PRACTISE method, and if you fail to get in, a FLICK, FLIP or throat JAB would automatically come to your rescue.

The attack by a dog would be met by the UPPER CUT from a CIRCLING GUARD. This covers the portion of one's person most liable to attack by this species of opponent. The average man, knowing no better, raises his stick to strike, thereby exposing the parts the dog is making for. This brings to mind an incident, small in itself, but quite sufficient to demonstrate the great benefit one derives from a knowledge of how to employ a Walking Stick efficiently in self-defence. The writer one day saw a shepherd fast asleep, and for a mild joke touched him on the nose with his stick. Like a flash the shepherd's dog, hitherto unseen, flew in for a nip. The stick thereupon travelled in an UPPER CUT from master's nose straight to the snout of his faithful companion, and the attack was cut short. Take a cue from this and get familiar with the methods of employing your stick effectively. In an emergency you will do the right thing automatically and your stick may prove so useful on occasions. Failing one method taking effect, you have so many others to fall back on. The methods already demonstrated are by no means the limit of the possibilities of employing your stick. They merely give you the means of employment under certain stated circumstances. As Napoleon said: "No genius suddenly or secretly reveals to me what I should do under circumstances which are to others unexpected; it is reflection and meditation beforehand." So take a leaf out of his book and be prepared for circumstances which will show an opponent that you have not been behindhand in acquiring a knowledge of how to defend your person.

Before we pass on to the next chapter, which deals with the training of organised bodies, and, therefore, is beyond the range of the average person, it would be as well to summarise here a few final reminders:—

1. Cultivate speed in all methods.
2. Get into all guards like a flash; similarly deliver all Cuts.
3. Do not forget to acquire the habit of guarding head and hand, and after every cut cover head and hand with HEAD GUARD in case opponent may have guarded your cut and replied to your head. Speed is the essence of this system of self-defence, so cultivate it.
4. Employ your SURPRISE PACKETS as speedily as you can.
5. Failing the opportunity of employing an efficient guard, jump into an opponent; you will thus minimise the

force of the blow aimed at you, and either end of your stick is bound to get home before you part company, for you know the "Soft Spots" and the method of getting there very much better than he is possibly aware of.

6. Last, but by no means least, you must above all things impress on your opponent from the start your formidable qualifications; and in all probability you will perforce be obliged to employ, if you catch him, a means you have hitherto not been instructed in—your boot!

CHAPTER XII

THE TRAINING OF ORGANISED BODIES

This chapter pertains more to the training of organised bodies of men such as Military, Police, Boy Scouts and other bodies subjected to discipline. The average person may, however, gather many useful tips of the manner of carrying out the instructions given in this book.

The initial instruction of a force of men must be by the "Snowball" system; starting with a few well trained, intelligent instructors. Not more than two or three selected men should be given to each instructor for training. When the course is completed, this increased number of trained men should be put on to train more men, and so on. Instruction must be individual; personal instruction is an indispensable factor. These methods are scientific, and any attempt to carry out the methods by any words of command which might be devised, must not be attempted.

Experience has shown that the average man takes very readily to this form of training. Perhaps this is accounted for by the realisation that he is acquiring a means of self-defence which will be of use to him both on and off duty. The personal element enters very largely into the training and gives a double interest, official and private.

Commence instruction by making each man in turn, get in front of a mirror (Fig. 52) and, from the ON GUARD position, practise Exercises laid down in the first chapter.

FIG. 52

FIG. 53

These Exercises must be persisted in till they are smoothly carried out as if the joints were working in well oiled bearings. They are of vital importance, as proficiency in all subsequent movements depends on the skill with which they have been executed. The men will naturally feel awkward for the first few lessons, but the ease with which they can be performed will quickly be obvious. The Exercises should be carried out slowly at first. Speed will come with practise. It is desirable to emphasise the fact here again that all the Exercises are devised, not only to cultivate a supple wrist, elbow and shoulder, etc., but are actually the motions to be gone through when delivering the various Cuts, and CIRCLING GUARDS (by means of which UPPER CUTS are delivered) and, unless a man can carry them out efficiently, he cannot go forward with the course of instruction. Assiduous practise is therefore essential.

On the men having attained proficiency in free and easy play with the stick individually, an instructor should commence a lesson by taking each pupil in turn and running through all guards and cuts (Fig. 53). Practise standing near to commence with and later at a distance, necessitating a lunge, when delivering cut.

Do not forget, when employing GUARDS, to step in to opponent so that the force of his blow is minimised.

The men should be gradually introduced to all methods until they reach the stage where they have the "Grand Combination" of all methods at their disposal when active practise can be carried out on the following lines:—

1. Advance on sack as illustrated in Fig. 54, employing CIRCLING GUARDS, and when within striking distance of sack, run through all cuts with a lunge. Cut to be of a glancing or wiping nature, and back into ON GUARD position after every cut. From CIRCLING GUARD also practise FLICKS and FLIPS on board, as shown in illustration roughly representing a man.

2. After cuts on sack are properly executed, combine cut with CROSS GUARD CUT LEFT at sack, finish up in CROSS GUARD, and reply again to sack from this position, body swinging round with cut.

3. Practise CLEARING PRACTISE in circle of sacks (Fig. 55). Let shoulder be the motive power, jerking it round with the cuts, and do not allow any flicking round of stick with the wrist. The Cuts must have a pull behind

FIG. 54

FIG. 55

FIG. 56

them. In this position practise double JABS with stick grasped in both hands and JABS delivered with upward tendency, left and right, employing both ends of stick in combination with shoulder.

4. Practise a combination of cuts by the CLEARING PRACTISE method with FLICKS and FLIPS, in the "Riot Enclosure" (Fig. 56). This enclosure is merely a circular arrangement of posts with sacks and boards irregularly placed to represent a mob, first row near, the second row looking over the front row's shoulder as it were. This makes for very active play with the stick. Commence practise by getting down into CLEARING PRACTISE cuts, FLICK in front, jump round to face about, deliver FLICK or FLIP; down again into CLEARING PRACTISE cuts, and carry on as above. This

FIG. 57
Recruits at Stick Play at a Police Headquarters in India.

FIG. 58
A Finished Squad.

FIG. 59
An Indian Boy Scout—trained to the use of the Walking Stick.

makes quite a spectacular show and fully demonstrates the high degree of efficiency that can be attained in Stick play when put to actual use, if the lines indicated in this book are carefully followed.

The employment of a stick in trench warfare, in accordance with the methods described, might prove of great service. It has certainly a wider range than the loaded cane which was employed so very extensively in the late war. The stick could also be used on duties where it might be undesirable or unnecessary to either carry or employ the rifle.

It will be at once seen that, in view of the essential element of speed required in all practises, and the numerous vulnerable parts exposed to attack, it would be impracticable to practise the methods by making the men set to with protective coverings. They would, in the first instance, be deprived of speed; and at the same time it would be beyond practical bounds to protect, for instance, a delicate portion like the knee, without impairing freedom of movement. In all practises, if the men are taught free and easy play with their sticks, and speed insisted on, and all cuts delivered on dummies, this is all that will be necessary. Experience has shown that men without any protective coverings acquire speed in GUARDS very much quicker than those taught with a mask; when, for instance, they are being put through the HEAD GUARDS. This is accounted for by the fact that the man without any covering knows he has only his GUARD to save him, and he is in consequence careful to acquire the habit of forming an efficient guard; whereas the man with the protective covering is not so careful, for he relies on his second line of defence, his mask!

Before concluding this book it might be advisable to state here for the benefit of those who may still be in doubt as to the efficiency of a Walking Stick as against a heavy cudgel, that the writer has taught strong supporters of the latter weapon who were, in their way, experts in its use. They commenced their course of instruction with little faith in the Walking Stick, but long before they completed their course they had entirely changed their opinion, and departed, after their course, renouncing for ever their former unwieldy weapon!

THE END.